Summ

Essentialism:

The Disciplined Pursuit of Less

By: Greg Mckeown

Proudly Brought to you by:

Legal & Disclaimer

Legal & Disclaimer

The information contained in this book is not designed to replace or take the place of any form of medicine or professional medical advice. The information in this book has been provided for educational and entertainment purposes only.

The information contained in this book has been compiled from sources deemed reliable, and it is accurate to the best of the Author's knowledge; however, the Author cannot guarantee its accuracy and validity and cannot be held liable for any errors or omissions. Changes are periodically made to this book. You must consult your doctor or get professional medical advice before using any of the suggested remedies, techniques, or information in this book. Images used in this book are not the same as of that of the actual book. This is a totally separate and different entity from that of the original book titled: "Essentialism: The Disciplined Pursuit of Less".

Upon using the information contained in this book, you agree to hold harmless the Author from and against any damages, costs, and expenses, including any legal fees potentially resulting from the application of any of the information provided by this guide. This disclaimer applies to any damages or injury caused by the use and application, whether directly or indirectly, of any advice or information presented, whether for breach of contract, tort, negligence, personal injury, criminal intent, or under any other cause of action.

You agree to accept all risks of using the information presented inside this book. You need to consult a professional medical practitioner in order to ensure you are both able and healthy enough to participate in this program.

Table of Contents

The Book at a Glance

Essentialism is for those who want to improve their productivity by dedicating what they have to what genuinely matters. It makes you reflect on what's really important to you and how you are using your valuable time and limited resources. This simple yet profound book teaches how to say "no" to trivialities to enable you to concentrate on the essentials in full force, so you can live your life according to your own decisions and arrive at the end of it with no regrets.

Chapter 1 explains the idea of Essentialism and why Non-essentialism is prevalent in modern society.

Part I describes the Essentialist's core mind-set and enumerates the three Non-essentialist assumptions and their Essentialist counterparts.

Chapter 2 is dedicated to the power of choice – why it matters to Essentialism and why people forget they have the ability to choose.

Chapter 3 focuses on the skill of discerning the few, essential things from the numerous, trivial ones.

Chapter 4 talks about trade-offs: in choosing one thing, we let go the others so we must decide wisely.

Part II chapters teach how to explore all possible options and decide the ones worth the choice.

Chapter 5 gives techniques on how to create valuable space to protect our energy and ability to make smart decisions.

Chapter 6 lists strategies on how to see what we need to, especially during times when our view is clouded by the trivial.

Chapter 7 debunks misconceptions about play, expresses why playfulness is beneficial for Essentialism and productivity, and provides suggestions on how to incorporate fun in daily living.

Chapter 8 corrects the false notion that sleeping less leads to greater productivity and offers several reasons why it increases it instead.

Chapter 9 presents pointers on setting criteria that help us select Essentials.

Part III is dedicated to the elimination of the Non-essential.

Chapter 10 highlights the importance of clarity in determining what's essential and presents instructions on how to be clear on essential matters.

Chapter 11 tackles the difficulties of saying "no" to the Non-essential and imparts strategies to make it easier.

Chapter 12 offers insights on why it's hard to let go Non-essential things and activities that we've invested in and imparts techniques to make the task more bearable.

Chapter 13 compares the process of eliminating non-essentials to the valuable yet underappreciated task of editing.

Chapter 14 discusses why setting boundaries is liberating instead of restricting.

Part IV is dedicated to making the execution of Essentialism close to effortless.

Chapter 15 is about creating buffers to protect one's self from the unexpected.

Chapter 16 gives doable action steps for removing obstacles that hamper efficiency.

Chapter 17 focuses on how to make small wins that eventually lead to big successes.

Chapter 18 deals with creating routines that facilitate the effortless execution of smart plans.

Chapter 19 links productivity to the ability to stay focused in the present.

Chapter 20 leaves us with the crucial lesson that Essentialism is not something that is done but something you become.

FREE BONUSES

P.S. Is it okay if we overdeliver?

Here at Readtrepreneur Publishing, we believe in overdelivering way beyond our reader's expectations. Is it okay if we overdeliver?

Here's the deal, we're going to give you an extremely condensed PDF summary of the book which you've just read and much more…

What's the catch? We need to trust you… You see, we want to overdeliver and in order for us to do that, we've to trust our reader to keep this bonus a secret to themselves? Why? Because we don't want people to be getting our exclusive PDF summaries even without buying our books itself. Unethical, right?

Ok. Are you ready?

Firstly, remember that your book is code: "**READ24**".

Next, visit this link: http://bit.ly/exclusivepdfs

Everything else will be self explanatory after you've visited: http://bit.ly/exclusivepdfs.

We hope you'll enjoy our free bonuses as much as we enjoyed preparing it for you!

Chapter 1. The Essentialist

True to its theme, the book starts at Chapter 1 with no long-winded introduction. The first few paragraphs describe a Silicon Valley executive's experiences with Essentialism. A larger business acquired his company and he found himself overworked, and at the same time he was offered a chance to retire early. Despite this, he didn't want to give up working yet so he asked his mentor what to do.

His mentor told him to stay and do what he could as a consultant, but he shouldn't do anything else that was not requested of him. This advice made him apprehensive at first because he used to do a lot for others, but he decided to go with it. He began to turn down requests that he can't fulfill with his available resources and time. This disappointed people at first, but to his surprise, their respect for him actually grew.

Because he was emboldened by people's responses, he applied stricter criteria when evaluating requests. He considered whether a request was the most important task he should be doing with the time and resources he currently has. Minimizing his actions this way also led to positive results.

Eventually, he was doing fewer things, but he did what was important really well. As he focused on crucial activities and stopped doing unimportant things, he gained more time for family and leisure. But not only that, he also gained some of the biggest bonuses of his entire career because of high-quality work.

It turns out that the advice of his mentor deals with Essentialism. The Essentialist's way is the consistent disciplined pursuit of fewer but better things. It is about pausing frequently to ask whether you are dedicating yourself to the right activities.

The fact is that there are far more opportunities and activities than what we could invest in. Among these, there may be several good options, but the majority of them are trivial and not vital. The Essentialist's job is to know the difference and select only the important choices.

The book shows an illustration of two circles that represent energy supply. The left circle has small arrows radiating from it in all directions. The second one has a large arrow pointing in one direction. The message is that choosing one thing to pool your energy unto will take you further than when you scatter your efforts among disparate endeavors.

Being an essentialist means you have to say "no" even when you are accustomed to saying "yes" just to appease others. It makes you live according to your own design and not by default or other people's demands. Instead of choosing reactively, an Essentialist selects the crucial few apart from the trivial many. He/she also does away with the nonessential and eliminates obstacles so that the important matters can flow more easily.

There are many non-essentialists nowadays because we generally have more options than ever before, are faced with social pressure, and believe that we can do everything. Aside from this, there is a cycle that causes successful people to be distracted by the non-essentials. At first, they become recognized because they have clear purposes that they dedicate their efforts to. Their good reputation encourages others to demand more of them, thus their energy becomes distributed across several tasks. This depletes them and makes them lose their focus, which may ultimately cause them to fail.

Essentialism is a method for EXPLORING where your "highest point of contribution" is, ELIMINATING things that do not contribute much (even those that seem to be good opportunities), and setting up a system that makes the

EXECUTION of actions almost effortless. Each of these three steps will be tackled fully by the next chapters.

The highest point of contribution is at the intersection of the right thing, the right reason and the right time. In comparison, the highest point of frustration is at the middle of everything popular that demands your immediate response. By giving ourselves the permission to be more selective with our actions, we break free from other people's control and we can discover our highest point of contribution – or, where we can do things that matter the most.

Part I. Essence: What is the Core Mind-Set of an Essentialist?

Conquer these assumptions to become an Essentialist:

1. I must do it
2. They are all important
3. I can fit all of these in my schedule

Replace the assumptions above with core truths:

1. I choose to do it
2. Only a few of these truly matter so I must select carefully
3. I can do something but not all things, and there are trade-offs

These three truths will free you and enable you to go for what actually matters to you.

Chapter 2. CHOOSE: The Invisible Power of Choice

What will you do if you can only do one thing in your life? Greg Mckeown asked himself this question one day, and he was shocked to find out that being in law school was not it. He has taken up law because somebody else told him to do so, and he thought it was a good idea since he could take on several jobs related to law. He studied all day and read all night, but he noticed that he wasn't succeeding in anything that he did. After realizing that he wasn't happy with the path he has chosen, he quit law after a few weeks.

A friend in America invited him to his wedding, so he left England and went there. He credits this decision for the creation of the book. His friend said that if he decided to come, and this statement struck him. He realized he had a choice but he just abandoned his ability to choose. Intellectually, he knew that he can decide not to go to law school, but emotionally, he felt that he just had to take up law. By rejecting the option not to go there, he was forced into something that wasn't really meaningful for him by default.

On the bright side, this experience changed his perspective about choices. Back then, he saw options as things and not as actions. They are not possessions, but activities. More importantly, he realized that people may not be in control of the options that become available for them, but they always are in charge of how they select among them.

The Essentialist knows the importance of his/her power to choose. He/she understands that people can choose because they have free will, but sometimes they just forget that they have it. He/she knows that when the right to choose is given up, other people will dictate the person's choices.

People can forget their ability to choose because of learned helplessness. An experiment done by Steve Maier and Martin Seligman demonstrated this concept. They got some dogs and put them in three groups; the first group received electrical shocks but they were given a lever to stop the shocks. The second group got a lever that didn't work. The third didn't get any shocks at all.

Afterwards, the dogs were placed in a huge box that had a low divider at its middle. One side was electrified while the other was not. It turned out that the dogs who were not shocked or had a lever to stopped the shocks learned to jump to the safe side of the box, but interestingly, the dogs that were electrocuted and had no way to halt the shocks didn't attempt to go away from the shocks. They thought that they couldn't do anything about their situation so they didn't try to save themselves.

Likewise, people who thought they had no choice often do not seek other options. They can stop trying to succeed, or they can push themselves too much that they overwork themselves. It's important to remember that we all have free will so that we don't learn to become helpless. This knowledge is crucial in becoming an Essentialist.

Chapter 3. DISCERN: The Unimportance of Practically Everything

Working harder to get more results may seem like the right thing to do, but there is often a point when increasing efforts will not lead anywhere and may even cause our downfall.

Greg Mckeown recalls that when he was young, he delivered newspapers to earn a pound one day in one hour. He thought that at that rate, it will take a long time to buy the MicroMachine he wanted, so he washed cars instead. He washed 3 cars per day and charged 2 pounds for each, and this also took an hour. Thus, he no longer earned 1 pound per hour but 6. This taught him a valuable lesson that some kinds of effort produce higher rewards than other kinds.

When he was in college, he worked in a coaching company and got 9 dollars an hour. This time, he didn't evaluate the jobs in terms of the ratio between the time it took to work and the rewards he obtained, but he considered the relationships between the time and the results he accomplished. This led him to ask what result will have the most value in his work – in this case, he focused on persuading clients to stay with the company. Soon enough, nobody cancelled and he earned a lot more.

Working hard is indeed valuable, but efforts do not always lead to better results. Doing less, but better is the key. The Pareto Principle says 20% of efforts create 80% of the results. Joseph Moses Juran, the author of Quality-Control Handbook, tested this principle in Japan. He taught Japanese to channel their energy in improving the few crucial features of their products, and this gradually led to the immense improvement of Japanese-made items. Warren Buffet credits 90% of his riches to only 10 investments. He filters out investment opportunities, says "no" to the majority of them, but invests big on the few that passes his standards.

A Non-essentialist mistakenly believes that almost all things are essential, while an Essentialist knows that almost everything is non-essential. Let go of the notion that any kind of effort will lead to a good result.

Take your time exploring all your options. This extra time is worth it because some matters are so important that they pay back the effort put into finding them several times. Even opportunities that seem to be good will be far less valuable than the truly great ones. As an essentialist, you must discern more so that you can do more.

Chapter 4. TRADE-OFF: Which Problem Do I Want?

Southwest Airlines made it a point to provide low fares by only travelling from point to point and not offering meals and high-class service. At first, many complained about the way they did business, but as time went by, more and more appreciated the low prices and the company generated a lot of profit. Continental Airlines tried to imitate them through Continental Lite, but since they can't let go of their original strategies, they spent their resources too thinly until the quality of their services deteriorated. They lost millions of dollars and became the target of thousands of complaints.

Continental Airlines learned the hard lesson of disregarding trade-offs this way. Aside from organizations, it also happens among individuals. For example, those who know that going to a meeting that's about to start in 10 minutes will take exactly 10 minutes, but they still do unnecessary things like checking their e-mail. There are also some who say they can go to a birthday party at a certain hour but they had previously bought tickets that are showing at the same hour of the party.

Many are deluded that they can do conflicting things at the same time. Essentialists acknowledge that there are trade-offs and they must choose among them. They know that saying "yes" to one opportunity requires saying "no" to several others. Despite this, they see it as a natural part of living and not something bad. They do not ask themselves what they have to give up but they ponder on what they want to go full force on. This change of thought can lead to profound effects.

Trade-offs should not be ignored just to avoid letting go of options. Not choosing may cause negative consequences. Options and priorities should be chosen deliberately and strategically so they will not be selected by default.

Part II. Explore: How Can We Discern the Trivial Many from the Vital Few?

It may seem as Essentialists are limiting themselves too much, but in fact, they usually explore more choices than Non-essentialists. The latter easily get excited by many things and pursue them straight away, and because they're so busy with them already, they explore less. Essentialists invest time thinking, questioning, and exploring. This is done not as an end but to distinguish the important few from the unimportant many.

Chapter 5. ESCAPE: The Perks of Being Unavailable

To distinguish the vital few from the useless many, we must have our space. In modern times, we don't get that space unless we deliberately seek it. What usually happens is that we become too busy with trivialities that we can't look at the bigger picture anymore. As an example, a leader stayed in his company for five years more than he wanted just because he was too preoccupied to decide whether he really needs to be there.

The Non-essentialist is so busy that he/she can't think where his/her life is heading, while the Essentialist deliberately creates space so he/she can explore life without being distracted. You can make space through the following ways:

Space to design

Greg Mckeown shares that he used to work at Stanford's Hasso Plattner Institute of Design, which has a soundproof and windowless enclosure called Booth Noir. Since this area is entirely free of distractions, students go there only to think and regain focus.

Like choices are not things but actions, the focus is not a thing but something that is done. Therefore, to have the focus, you must escape to the focus.

The focus is not obsessing about something, but exploring possibilities and answering questions. It is not fixating on one thing, but adjusting one's perspective constantly.

You must have a space to create your design. Find a place you can go to that is free of distractions so you can create your thinking space.

Space to concentrate

Greg Mckeown knows an intelligent, yet constantly distracted, executive who isolated himself for eight weeks in a motel without the Internet to finish a huge project. He observed that the executive knew his highest point of contribution required a space for focused thought, but he was a bit sad that the latter needed to go to extreme measures for it.

It's interesting that great minds had taken a similar approach that the executive did. To give an example, Isaac Newton was in near complete solitary confinement for 2 years as he worked on the Principia Mathematica which described the three laws of motion and universal gravitation. He thought about what he wrote continually and to the exclusion of other things.

Greg Mckeown was inspired by what Newton did so he blocked 8 hours per day to write his book. He didn't answer calls and emails or went to meetings from 5 am to 1 pm. He calls this his monk-mode and it gave him space that enabled him to write more quickly and spend the rest of his time wiser.

Setting aside time to think is not the five minutes that you scribble on your to-do list or daydreaming about how to tackle your project. It is setting a distraction-free period in a distraction-free place for nothing else other than thinking.

The busier you are, the more that you need to escape to think. The good thing is that no matter how busy you are, you can always carve some time and space for reflecting. LinkedIn CEO Jeff Weiner sets 2 hours for pondering the essential questions, recharging himself, and entering a coaching mindset.

On your calendar, plot a schedule for thinking about the big picture and what you often think about. Use this time to do nothing other than think.

Space to read

Bill Gates takes an entire week off just to read, and he did this even during the most frantic moments of Microsoft's history. If a week seems too long for you, you can just schedule some time for reading during the day, preferably within 20 minutes of waking up. Use this time for reading classical literature and not the latest news, books, or emails. Reading will help you overcome the urge to check your social media notifications or mail as soon as you open your eyes. It will also prevent you from lunging into the activities that face you and give you a broader perspective of what you really have to do.

Chapter 6. LOOK: See What Really Matters

Were you ever uncertain about what you must zone into? Was there a time where you were overwhelmed by so much information that you don't know how to handle it? Have you missed something in your home or work and you didn't recognize your error until you can't do anything about it? If you answered "yes", this next Essentialist method is for you:

You must stop hyperfocusing on the minor details and view the bigger scene.

Eastern Air Lines Flight 401 crashed on December 29, 1972, even though nothing major was wrong in with the plane. What happened was that the officers were too focused on an indicator light that didn't work as expected. Because their attention was directed towards that malfunctioning light, they didn't notice that the autopilot was deactivated and they were already flying too low. This caused the plane to crash into the Florida Everglades.

Determining what is important requires discipline in scanning and filtering conflicting and competing information, options, opinions, and facts that clamor for your attention. It doesn't mean hearing only the loudest, but finding the point of the discussion and noticing what's not being talked about.

These things will help you see what you need to see:

Keep a journal. Memory is selective so you might not remember everything that you need. Writing things down helps you keep track of what you might forget. Begin journaling with short sentences instead of novel-length passages so you won't be burned out. Every 3 months, spend 1 hour to browse through what you wrote so far. Don't focus too much on the specific details of your entries, but notice patterns in your experiences. Think about what you can change to improve your life.

Go personally into your field and fully explore issues. A group was tasked to design an incubator that costs 1% of its original cost to save premature babies in developing countries. They first made a low-cost incubator, but when they visited Nepal, they noticed that most babies were born in homes that lack electricity. This taught them that giving cheap incubators will not solve the problem since they won't work without electricity. Instead, they decided to create an incubator with a wax-like material that can be heated by hot water. If they didn't go there, they never would have learned what they needed to. Thus, you should go beyond researching and evaluate developments yourself so you can come up with solutions that actually solve problems.

Notice unusual and abnormal details. When you encounter a story, dig more deeply. Analyze information related to the story and determine what its place in the bigger picture is. Consider sides that other people have overlooked if there are. Place yourself in the shoes of different individuals so you can get fresh perspectives.

Be clear on what question you are trying to answer. If you observe politicians closely, you will notice that they are good at evading questions while pretending to have answered it. Don't be like them. Ask and answer tough questions. When you're brainstorming, remember the question you are trying to seek answers to. If someone asks you something, get to the inquiry's essence to give back the right data and come up with an effective action plan.

Chapter 7. PLAY: Embrace the Wisdom of Your Inner Child

Playing is natural to children – when we were young, no one taught us how to play; we just did it because it was fun. When we grew older, we were told that playing is trivial and reserved only for kids. The school system removed leisure from learning, and it can hinder students' creativity. In addition, most organizations and companies do not encourage a playful culture in the workplace, so by adulthood, most people have severely decreased their ability to explore and imagine.

Greg Mckeown defines play as something done simply for fun and not as a means to an end. It seems to be unnecessary, but it is in truth essential because:

It can improve a lot of things in life such as one's health, relationships, learning, adaptability, and capacity to innovate. It even enhances the brain's plasticity or ability to upgrade itself.

It counteracts stress, which deteriorates productivity. Stress literally shuts down the parts of our brain that help us become inquisitive, creative explorers. When playing, we can think more clearly and remain calm.

It makes us more creative and gives us more options. It makes us notice more possibilities and create more connections. It helps produce new ideas and view old ones with fresh eyes. It opens up our mind and perspective. It encourages us to challenge assumptions and be more welcoming of new notions. It enables us to expand our consciousness and compose our own stories.

Play amplifies the brain's executive functions, which include deciding, prioritizing, anticipating, planning, scheduling, and analyzing. It stimulates both logical reasoning and creative exploration. Columbus, Newton, Watson and Crick, and Einstein came up with their brilliant ideas while they were actively playing. Shakespeare and Mozart were said to be constantly in a playful mood.

Some companies like Twitter, IDEO, Pixar, and Google encourage playfulness in their environments through whimsical decorations and toys. These greatly helped those who work in their function at their best.

To have more play in your own life, remember what you did when you were a child. What gave you happiness and excitement? How can you relive that in your current situations? Play is essential, so go ahead and enjoy.

Chapter 8. SLEEP: Protect the Asset

You are your asset. If you don't invest adequately in yourself, in your body, mind, and spirit, you damage the asset that will help you make your highest contribution. A common way to do this is by not sleeping enough.

The Non-essentialists consider sleep as a burden. The Essentialists know that sleep is needed to function at high levels of contribution. It's not a luxury, but a priority. It does not cause laziness but it can spur creativity. Sleep protects the ability to prioritize, a crucial factor of Essentialism.

Non-essentialists think that losing one hour of sleep means gaining one hour of productivity. Essentialists know that one hour of sleep equates to several hours of better productivity. This is why they deliberately and systematically include sleep in their productive schedules so they can explore, do, and achieve more.

During sleep, your brain encodes and restructures information, so if you don't sleep, you will find it harder to learn and solve problems. Sleeping will enhance your capacity to make connections, explore, and do things in better ways. If you're trying to master a skill, you will get more out of your practices if you are well-rested.

Sleep is essential because it leads to better health, creativity, and productivity. Don't neglect sleep because it allows you to function at your best and do more things faster. Sleep at least 8 hours and take naps during the day when you need to.

Chapter 9. SELECT: The Power of Extreme Criteria

It's not a choice between just "yes" and "no", but "absolutely yes" and "definitely no". Your closet can get full of clothes that you don't wear because you think you might wear them someday. If you ask yourself if you really like the clothes before keeping them, you can eliminate clutter and gain more space for essential items. We can do this with choices of all kinds.

Apply the 90% rule to decisions and dilemmas. When you think about an option, consider the one most crucial criterion for that choice, then score it between zero and a hundred percent. If you give it lower than 90% then change it to 0 and discard it right away. This will stop you from being stuck in indecision or at deciding among those choices that you gave a 60 – 70. You can also use a scoring of 1 to 10 if you prefer. Keep those that you gave 9 to 10 and reject everything else.

This Essentialist skill of selection requires acknowledging trade-offs. Having selective criteria is a trade-off in itself – at times, you must turn down a good option because a better one might arrive. The option may or may not come, but by applying the criteria allows you to define what perfect option to look for instead of letting circumstances or others choose it for you.

Assigning numbers makes you choose rationally and consciously rather than emotionally and impulsively. Even if it takes more discipline to have tough criteria, it is necessary. If you decide following unspoken criteria such as doing something simply because somebody asked you to do it, or because everybody else is doing it, then you might find yourself toiling away at nonessential activities.

Non-essentialists always say "yes" to requests and opportunities while Essentialists say "yes" only to the top 10%. The former abides by broad, unspoken criteria while the latter applies narrow and explicit criteria. Being selective and explicit of what options to take will create a systematic tool that helps discern the essential and eliminate those that are not. This will also help you gather relevant information to make informed decisions.

Being selective doesn't only mean picking the opportunities to pursue, but also saying "no" to some opportunities that come to you. Avoid saying "yes" just because it gives you a quick reward – agreeing to it puts you at risk of saying "no" to a more meaningful opportunity.

This is a simple process that will help you sift through opportunities:

Write down what the opportunity is.

Write at least three minimum standards that the options must pass to be considered. You can only consider the opportunity if it meets these criteria.

Write three ideal or extreme criteria for the same option. If the opportunity did not meet the first set of minimum requirements, then you should decline it. However, it should also pass 2 out of three extreme criteria or else you should reject it.

A Google search with more specific keywords will give you fewer search results. Similarly, applying highly specific criteria will help you narrow down your options. When deciding between big decisions, ask where your passion is, what makes use of your talents, and what meets an important need in the world today. This is where your highest point of contribution exists.

PART III: ELIMINATE: HOW CAN WE CUT OUT THE TRIVIAL MANY?

Part three is about eliminating non-essentials in order to make a higher contribution towards vital things. You can imagine this as letting go of the pile of clothes that you've set aside as clutter. Aside from determining what efforts and actions don't add to your highest contribution, you will still have to actively remove these. Doing this concentrates your energy to vital matters and makes you gain other people's respect.

It may be hard to let go of old clothes and other possessions, but this is normal. According to studies, people put higher value on what they own than what they are really worth, so it's more difficult to get rid of them. To overcome this tendency, ask yourself how much you would spend on something if you don't already own it. For an opportunity, ask what you are willing to do to acquire it if you didn't have it.

When you have adequately explored your choices, do not ask yourself what to say "yes" to, but what you should say "no" to. This will reveal your authentic priorities. Remember that when you fail to say "no" to something not important, you actually say "yes" to it.

Chapter 10. CLARIFY: One Decision That Makes a Thousand

Essentialism involves eliminating any action or activity that is not aligned with what you're planning to accomplish. For this, you must clarify your purposes and intentions.

When a team is unclear about their purpose, roles, and goals, they will most likely experience stress, confusion, and frustration, which then cause them to become less cooperative. But, when these things are clear, the team members are motivated to perform well together.

Not having clarity of purpose makes individuals waste energy and time to the trivial many. When there is enough clarity, they can produce innovations and attain breakthroughs.

There are many ways to lose clarity. People can become distracted by politics. When team members hyperfocus on winning the approval of the boss, each of them may make up their own rules, waste energy on making themselves look better, and echoing the boss' ideas. In our own lives, without a clear idea of our values and aspirations, we may also spend so much in acquiring non-essentials and boosting our self-importance, which causes us to neglect essential activities like taking care of our own health and spending quality time with friends and family.

Teams that have no purpose lose their leader. They push their short-term interests and have little to no awareness of how their actions affect the long-term goals of the whole team, so they set themselves back. Although each may have good intentions, when people are working on disparate tasks, they do not add to the team's highest level of contribution and they may even derail the entire group's progress. Just the same, individuals who are engaged in too many disparate activities may fail to accomplish their essential goal.

To achieve clarity of purpose individually and in teams, one thing to do is have an essential intent. Essential intents are concrete, inspirational, measurable, and meaningful. It is what settles thousands of decisions later on, even for decades after the initial choice.

Non-essentialists have vague mission statements, but essentialists have an inspirational and concrete strategy. Non-essentialists discuss concrete objectives that don't inspire, while essentialists have intents that are memorable and meaningful. Non-essentialists have values, but no principles for demonstrating them, while Essentialists makes an important decision that eliminates several later decisions.

Essential intents don't need to be formulated elegantly because it is not the style that matters, but the substance. After all, they are about deciding and not creating elaborate statements. Ask the essential question "if you could be excellent at just one thing, what is it?" Aside from this, ask how you will know when you've successfully accomplished your intent. Being specific with your intent will make it more real and more inspiring.

Coming up with an essential intent is difficult. It requires insight, courage, and foresight to know which efforts and activities will add to your highest point of contribution. You must ask hard questions, make real trade-offs, and exercise discipline to weed out competing priorities that take your focus away from your true intention. It is worth all the effort because organizations, teams, and individuals can fully achieve excellence when they have a clear purpose.

Chapter 11. DARE: The Power of a Graceful "No"

Saying "no" can change history. A good example is when Rosa Parks refused to stand up in the bus; that simple act of defiance triggered the civil rights movement. She didn't say "no" because she was normally confident – in fact, she became secretary to the president of the NAACP because she was asked to and she was too shy to refuse. However, her historic refusal came from a passionate conviction that she will not be humiliated anymore.

We can emulate Rosa Parks' conviction when we must hold on to the essential despite being socially pressured to give way to the nonessential. Were you ever split between what you know is right and what someone else is forcing you to do? Have you said "yes" even if you didn't mean it just to avoid angering or disappointing others? Handling these situations is a major skill you must learn to become an Essentialist. It is also among the hardest to master since it requires courage.

It's natural not to want to disappoint the others, but if you keep on saying "yes" because of it, you will miss the important things. The difficulty of immediately choosing what's important from what's not is caused by being clear on what the essentials are. This causes us to be vulnerable. In comparison, clarity about them shields us from non-essentials that come to us and provides us with the strength to say "no" to them.

Peter Drucker, who in Greg Mckeown's view, is the father of modern management, once turned down Mihaly Csikszentmihalyi's invitation for an interview even though he greatly admired his work. It's because he believes that productivity depends on the ability to say "no" to things that further other people's agendas instead of one's own. This earned Csikszentmihalyi's admiration and he wrote about his response in his book.

Non-essentialists say "yes" all the time to avoid pressure and awkwardness; Essentialists say "no" to non-essentials firmly but gracefully. Here is how:

Consider the decision and the relationship as separate from each other. Denying the request is different from denying the requester, so you don't have to feel too bad about it.

Saying "no" doesn't mean actually saying the word. You could say something like, "I'm happy you thought of me but I'm already overcommitted."

Focus on trade-offs. Think about what you're giving up when you say "yes" so it will become easier to respond "no".

Be aware of what the other is trying to sell you. This will make you consciously decide whether to buy it.

Accept that saying "no" means trading popularity for respect. Although the person you turned down may be mad or disappointed at first, he/she will respect you more once the negative emotions wear off. This can be worth it since respect is more valuable than popularity in the long run.

Remember that giving a clear "no" can be better than a vague "yes". Agreeing to do something even if you know you won't do it is more annoying than saying "no" outright.

Greg Mckeown gives a repertoire of saying "no":

Pause. This works when you are face to face with someone. Silently count from one to three before responding. Don't be controlled by silence; use it.

Say "no", but. Greg got an e-mail of an invitation to coffee, but he was busy writing his book at that time. He replied that he was consumed with writing as of the moment but he would meet the person once the book was done. You can also say "no" over e-mail because you can put some thought into how to phrase your rejection, and your recipient may also take it more easily because e-mail is more distant than a rejection said personally.

Say that you will check your calendar and get back to the person. This will help you see whether you are already overbooked or not instead of cramming the new demand in your schedule.

Set e-mail bouncebacks. This will tell them that you can't respond for a given period of time, and not that you don't like talking with them. When Greg Mckeown did this when he was in Monk Mode, he recalled that people adapted to his short absence quite well.

Ask what to deprioritize. When you can't directly say "no", especially when you're talking with your boss, ask what you should deprioritize to focus on the new requirement. Otherwise, say that you won't be able to work well on a job you're proud of if you also took the new task.

Use humor. People will accept rejection better if you make them laugh. Greg Mckeown was invited to train for a marathon; he flatly said "no" but his friend found it funny. For him, it was proof that Mckeown was indeed practicing what he was preaching.

Phrase "no" as: You can do X and I'm willing to do Y. Example: You may borrow the car, and I'm willing to give you my keys. This implies that you won't drive for the person.

Reply: I can't do it but X may be interested. It may be tempting to imagine that your help is particularly important, but in most cases, others don't really care who does it for as long as they receive the help they needed.

Say "no" to the unimportant so you can say "yes" to the things that truly matter. Like Tom Friel, Heidrick & Struggles' former CEO has said, you must learn to say "yes" slowly and "no" quickly. Essentialists accept the fact that they cannot please all people every time. Saying "no" reasonably, respectfully, and gracefully will cost you socially but only for the short term.

Chapter 12. UNCOMMIT: Win Big by Cutting Your Losses

Sunk-cost bias makes a person keep on investing energy, money or time into a thing that is a losing proposition just because he/she had already paid for a cost that can't be repaid.

This bias is what keeps people holding on to non-essentials and things that are not benefitting them. Henry Gribbohm spent all of his life savings in a carnival game in the hopes of winning an Xbox Kinect. He reports that the more cash he spent, the stronger his determination to win became. He was obsessed in winning his cash back that he found it harder and harder to leave the game.

A Non-essentialist can't let go of traps such as those created by the sunk-cost bias. An Essentialist is brave and confident enough to admit errors and uncommit no matter how much the sunk costs are.

A Non-essentialist doesn't want to stop because he/she has already invested so much. The Essentialist thinks about how much he/she will invest if he/she wasn't already invested in it.

A Non-essentialist holds on to the thought that if he/she keeps trying, he/she can make it work. The Non-essentialist ponders what else he/she can do with the resources that become available when he/she stops committing.

Greg Mckeown gives tips on avoiding being trapped into commitment:

Be careful of the endowment effect. This is the tendency to value what you own more than what it's actually worth. In an experiment led by Daniel Kahneman, half of the subjects were given coffee mugs while the rest didn't get any. When the researchers asked the first group how much they will sell the mugs, they said that they will sell it for no $5.25 and above, but the group without mugs is willing to pay only $2.25 to $2.75. Their conclusion was that ownership alone increases perceived value and makes owners less willing to part with owned items.

Pretend that you don't own the thing or opportunity yet. Don't focus too much on how you value the item right now, but consider how much you would pay to get it if you don't already own it. Instead of asking how you feel if you missed out on a particular opportunity, ask yourself how much you would actually sacrifice to obtain that opportunity. If you are involved with a failing project, ask how hard you would work for it if it was still new to you.

Once you've realized that you made a mistake with your choices, admit failure and stop forcing things to fit your preferences. Do not continue doing something just because you've always done so before. Constantly ask whether it is still worth to continue your investments; do not base it on history but on whether there is still a need for it.

Stop committing casually. Don't make a habit of agreeing to a request or offering your help just to be polite. Before speaking, pause and reflect on whether it's essential and you can follow through without sacrificing other things. In addition, experiment on what commitments or actions you can remove without creating a drastic impact. You can stop doing many things that you thought were absolutely necessary for others.

Chapter 13. EDIT: The Invisible Art

Editing is called the invisible art since not many people know that it is responsible for excellent creations. In the Academy Awards, two-thirds of movies that have been nominated for Best Film Editing have won Best Picture, and all of those that were given the Best Picture award also got good feedback regarding their editing. Despite this, according to Greg Mckeown, TV viewers do not focus on the winners of Best Film Editing, and only a few know about Michael Kahn, a film editor with several wins.

Mark Harris explains that a skilled film editor makes it difficult to not see the important because he/she eliminates everything except what absolutely needs to be there. Just as exploring can be compared to the job of a journalist, eliminating the non-essentials can be thought of as the editor's expertise.

An editor is not just someone who says "no" or eliminate. He/she is also someone who deliberately subtracts to add to the quality of a piece. Similarly, being an editor in your life helps amplify your level of contribution. It makes you gain focus and energy. It enables meaningful activities and relationships to grow.

Editing, a task involving the elimination of the irrelevant and unimportant, is an Essentialist activity. It supports the effortless execution of valuable tasks by subtracting anything that is unnecessary, distracting, or awkward.

The Non-essentialist believes that adding to something makes it better and he/she is attached to every detail. The Essentialist knows that improving something means subtracting to it, and he/she eliminates distracting details.

Here is how to edit your life:

Cut Options

When deciding, cutting options can be frightening, but it's the very essence of making decisions. In fact, the Latin root of the word decision, "cis/cid", means to kill or cut. Although it involves some sacrifice, it can lead to joy afterwards.

Condense

Condensing is expressing it as concisely and clearly as you can. This doesn't mean doing more simultaneously but wasting less. You must strive to lower the ratio of effort and results, words and ideas, and square feet and usefulness. You must also focus on the degree of meaning rather than the amount of activity – for instance, you can replace several meaningless activities with one highly meaningful activity.

Correct

An editor makes something correct. It can involve minor things such as correcting spelling or grammar or as crucial as fixing argument errors. For this, he/she must be in touch with the main purpose of the work he's trying to edit. Always keep your life's purpose in mind and compare it with your behaviors and activities. If they're not aligned with it, edit them.

Edit less

Becoming a good editor means knowing when to refrain from editing and let things be. After all, what makes a surgeon great is not his/her ability to make numerous incisions. Likewise, the best editors can be those that are restrained and non-intrusive. To be your life's editor, you must not only edit away the non-essentials; you must also edit your urge to be involved if you don't really need to.

A Non-essentialist sees editing as a task to be done only when things already overwhelm him/her. This is unfortunate because prolonging the editing may force him/her to perform huge cuts that are not always to his/her choosing. By cutting, condensing, and correcting part of the routine, the Essentialist can make minor but deliberate modifications that will help improve the overall quality of his/her life

Chapter 14. LIMIT: The Freedom of Setting Boundaries

Greg Mckeown considers our era as a Non-essentialist one where boundaries tend to disappear. He labels technology as one of the culprits for this, and through devices, people expect us to be available even during the times when we should be concentrating on family or work. Although companies may not be comfortable when employees bring family members with them, they often do not hesitate when they demand them to work during the weekends.

Boundaries are like sandcastle walls. When we allow one to topple, the rest crash down as well. Sometimes, setting boundaries come with a high price such as the possibility of losing a job or limiting one's career, but if you don't set boundaries, there will be none of them to protect you. Otherwise, the boundaries you manage to have will be set by another individual who may not have your best interests at heart, or by circumstances that you don't have any choice over.

Non-essentialists see boundaries as limits but Essentialists perceive it as things that remove their limits. Despite this, Non-essentialists also suffer when others attempt to make them do more than what they're capable of. To make matters worse, they exert a lot of effort to say "no" directly. The Essentialists, however, have planned for this so they have already set rules beforehand so they won't have to deal with the inconvenience of rejecting someone outright.

Essentialists draw strength from boundaries. They know that boundaries keep their valuable time from being trampled and it frees them from having to agree to things that support other people's objectives and not their own.

There will always be people who demand much of us and make their problems ours. When someone is draining your energy and time for their own sake, you must put up walls. This doesn't only mean at the time when they requested it, but you must have defenses early on by specifying your limits. This will help you disregard things that will waste your time and push your boundaries quickly

Solving others' problems when they should be the ones handling them is not helping; not only does it burden us, it also stunts their growth. This is like using a water sprinkler for your neighbor's yard instead of yours. He doesn't see any problem with his lawn but your grass is already dying. In the end, he becomes neglectful of his lawn and you end up with a dry one. Solving this requires that you set up a fence to rightfully keep your problems in your own yard and his problems in his yard.

Find your boundaries by recalling the times when you felt that your rights are trampled upon, or when you felt uncomfortable when somebody asked something from you. Think carefully about what you are willing to do for others and what you will never do unless it overlaps your plans and interests in some way. Communicating this with someone you work with early on will help prevent burdening each other with unwelcome requests.

PART IV: EXECUTE: HOW CAN WE MAKE DOING THE VITAL FEW THINGS ALMOST EFFORTLESS?

Non-essentialists force their execution of things, but Essentialists eliminate non-essentials by investing time to make execution effortless. The next chapters will teach how to do make the process as easy as possible.

Chapter 15. BUFFER: The Unfair Advantage

The Hebrew Bible tells the story of Joseph the Dreamer, who correctly interpreted the Pharaoh's dream that there will be 7 years of abundance and 7 years of famine. Joseph advised that they should keep a fifth of their harvest per year to supply them for the lean years ahead. Because of this, they were saved while the rest of those in Egypt went hungry. This describes another powerful Essentialist practice – setting up buffers or extra spaces.

Apart from famines and other extreme conditions, there are many other things that we should anticipate in this unpredictable world. The Essentialist plans and prepares for contingencies. He/she makes a buffer to prepare for the unexpected, so there is enough room when unforeseen things come up.

To illustrate the importance of buffers, Greg Mckeown describes driving a car. Each car should maintain as much space from the one in front of it as possible to avoid a collision. The other car may back up, change direction, or the car being driven may accelerate unintentionally – if there is little space between the two, they are sure to hit each other.

If we forget to observe buffers, we are forced to brake hard or swerve at the last moment. This often happens because commitments and projects tend to fill up the time that has been allocated to them.

The Non-essentialist assumes a best-case scenario and repeatedly underestimates the length of time something will be done. What actually happens is that they take longer, the task turns out to be complicated, and random things come up. These cause them to react to problems, and by doing so, they can't focus on the main task and their work quality plummets. They skip sleep, send their project incomplete, cut corners, or sometimes they just give up altogether.

When the Non-essentialist does things at the last moment, Essentialists prepares well ahead of time. They do not assume that things will happen the way they expect but they prepare for mishaps. They give themselves plenty of room for moving themselves to safety.

Apply extreme preparations. There were two teams that competed to be the first to go to the South Pole. Robert Falcon Scott, the first team's leader, assumed the best case scenario and didn't prepare adequately. Roald Amundsen brought 4 thermometers instead of 1, carried 3 tons of food, used 20 markers, and researched the trip thoroughly. The result was everyone in Scott's team died while Amundsen's team was victorious.

Add a 50% buffer to the time that you estimate to finish a project/task. The planning fallacy is the tendency to underestimate a task's duration even when you've done it before. Sometimes, we do know we can't do something quickly but we don't want to admit it, so we make wrong estimations of the time when we'll be done.

Plan for scenarios by asking these questions:

1. What are the risks you might face in this project?
2. What is this project's worst-case scenario?
3. What are the social effects of this?
4. What will the financial impact be?
5. How can you practically invest to minimize risks and strengthen your resilience socially and financially?

Essentialists accept that we can't fully prepare or anticipate for all possibilities so they create buffers for whatever might happen. The most successful companies are not those that were able to foresee the unexpected – they are those who had plenty of buffers and made good use of them.

Chapter 16. SUBTRACT: Bring Forth More by Removing Obstacles

Alex Rogo is a fictional character in a business parable. He was trying to solve problems in a plant he was working at but to no avail. The answer came to him when he was leading a group of Scouts during a hike. His group was scattered because the kids were walking at different paces. He figured out that placing the slowest at front and the fastest ones behind, they will meet at the middle. Although this worked, the group was walking at the slowest hiker's speed. What he did was he made the travel easier for the straggler – he lightened up his backpack by distributing the contents among the hikers. This greatly improved their overall speed so they made it back to their camp early. Alex applied the insights he gained from this experience to the plant. He found out the slowest machine and upgraded it. Soon enough, the plant's efficiency rose tremendously.

What do you consider as the "slowest hiker" in your life or work? What are the obstacles that are preventing you from attaining what is really important to you? Identify and remove these constraints systematically so you can reduce the friction that's stopping you from working on what's essential.

Essentialists don't use quick-fix solutions or zone into obvious or immediate challenges. They hunt the ones that are slowing down their progress. They don't do more in the hopes of fixing problems; they strategically find and remove obstacles so they will bring forth more of their desired results.

When specifying the "slowest hiker" you must remember that even productive activities like research, e-mailing individuals to gather information, or rewriting reports, can actually be obstacles. Again, you must be clear on what your essential intent is, align your actions with it, and know the specifics of your desired outcomes so you can measure your progress.

To minimize friction with someone else, use the "catch more flies with honey". Send an e-mail but go talk to him/her. Ask what his/her obstacles or bottlenecks are stopping him/her from attaining the goal, and how you can help remove them. Do not pester him/her but sincerely want to support him/her. You will get a warmer response instead of just sending another email with your demand that he/she work.

Getting rid of obstacles doesn't need to be effortful. Being smart about what to remove may be all that you need. It's like removing a boulder perched atop a hill – a slight push is all it takes to make it roll away.

Chapter 17. PROGRESS: The Power of Small Wins

The Essentialist doesn't try to accomplish everything simultaneously, but instead starts with small steps and makes progress. He/she doesn't go for large victories that don't have much importance, but he/she pursues small yet essential wins.

Progress is the most effective of all human motivators. A small win produces momentum and confirms that more successes are possible. After all, it's much harder to force a big win as compared to building up small wins that eventually carry you to where you want to go. In contrast, if you aim too high and fail to reach it, your disappointment may prevent you from trying harder next time.

You can choose to apply your energies to make execution of right actions easy or be resigned to a system that makes it more challenging to do what you know you must. These techniques will help you come up with a beneficial system:

Define your minimal viable progress. Ask yourself what smallest amount of progress is valuable and useful to the task you are attempting to accomplish. If you're a seller, ask what's the simplest product you can come up with that will be valuable and useful to the customer you have in mind. Start with the small things because this will build up your momentum. Let go of perfectionism because something done is infinitely better than something perfect that never gets accomplished.

Determine your minimal viable preparation. Accomplish deadlines and goals by beginning at the earliest possible moment with the minimal time investment. Investing as little as 10 minutes in your assignment or project two weeks before the deadline can spare you from cramming. Take an upcoming deadline or goal and figure out what the minimal amount you could do to prepare for it. Start "early and small" instead of doing it "late and big".

Reward your progress visually. Plot your progress, give yourself stars, or put a check mark next to your accomplished tasks. This will make your progress more tangible so you'll be more motivated to continue.

Chapter 18. FLOW: The Genius of Routine

The Non-essentialist executes important actions forcefully and lets non-essentials become the default. The Essentialist creates an effortless routine that makes achieving the essential as default. Although he/she works hard in some cases, with a routine set, each effort spent for it will yield greater results.

Routine is a powerful tool for eliminating obstacles. Without it, nonessential distractions become overwhelming. If we make a routine that protects the essentials, we will execute them automatically. We won't have to waste our energy repeatedly thinking about our priorities and deciding what the best thing to do is. We just have to initially spend some effort in creating a well-thought routine to follow and our actions will become the natural result of it.

Duke University researchers have found out that around 40% of choices are unconscious. We don't think about them, thus they present both risks and opportunities. On the positive side, we can acquire new abilities that gradually turn instinctive. On the downside, we may also develop counterproductive habits.

To focus upon the right routines:

- Overhaul triggers or change what your triggers mean to you so they cause you to do something better
- Create new triggers
- Accomplish the most essential action first especially when it's the most difficult
- Mix up routines, such as carry out different routines on different days
- Handle routines one at a time

Designing a routine requires brainpower at first, but it's worth it in the long term. A routine guides your actions so they will be aligned with your chosen purpose and prevents you from being sidetracked by temptations and distractions. It also removes the burden of having to think about what to do.

Chapter 19. FOCUS: What's Important Now?

Operating at the highest level of contribution means tuning in to what's important for the moment. Every second of worrying about what happened or what might happen distracts from what is essential at the present.

When obligations and tasks are competing for your focus, pause and get into the present moment. Ask yourself what's important at that very moment and not tomorrow or an hour later. If you're uncertain, list everything that's demanding your attention and cross out anything that's not immediately important.

The mind of the Essentialist is focused upon the present so he/she can tune in to what's important right at that moment. The Non-essentialist's focus wavers to the future and the past so he/she is plagued with worries and fear. By being more in control of where you put your awareness to, you can enjoy the moment more, and in freeing your mind from distractions and negative emotions, you will be able to accomplish more with the time you have.

To be more fully present in the now:

Specify the most important thing right now. The essentials are what you must focus on.

Stop thinking too much about the future. Even if there are essential tasks that you want to do someday, if they're not important right now, release them. List them down so you can do something about them when the time is right.

Prioritize. Use your time wisely by accomplishing essential tasks according to urgency.

The ancient Greeks called time by two names: Chronos and Kairos. Chronos is the chronological time that is measured by the clock, while Kairos are meaningful events. During the day, notice your Kairos moments. Record them in a journal. What triggered that Kairos moment and what made you leave it? Once you found what activated it, bring it back when you need to.

Chapter 20. BE: The Essentialist Life

You can think about Essentialism as something that you do sometimes or as something that involves who you are. The former is something to add to your already overcommitted life. The latter is a simpler way of doing it since it becomes your lifestyle.

When you become an Essentialist at the core, you will be more confident in your ability to pause, push the non-essentials away, and not rush in things you don't have to do. You will stop being other people's pawns. If you have been a Non-essentialist for a long time, you may find it difficult at first to adopt a new lifestyle, but the rewards will make you glad that you did.

An Essentialist's life is one that is lived without regrets. Identifying what matters and investing energy and time in it will mean that all actions are dedicated to what matters. As a result, nothing is wasted, and the desired outcomes are attained.

What is Essential to you? Once you answered this question, remove everything else. When you're ready to find your answers, you are ready to walk the path of the Essentialist.

Conclusion

The book *Essentialism* is created to address the deep need of people to live their lives to the fullest. It is the product of the author's reflections of what has happened to him and his thorough research on other people and their work. Although the Essentialist skills are discussed well, one will only become an Essentialist if he/she constantly lives it instead of considering it as a series of tasks that are done and eventually forgotten about.

Chapter 1 reminds us that it's easy to fall into the trap of Non-essentialism so we must always recognize what is truly essential for us.

In Part 1, we are reminded that we can't and don't have to do everything because our time, energy, and resources are limited. Instead, we must select what to do deliberately according to actual importance.

Chapter 2 alerts us that we often forget that we can choose a lot of things about our lives. We must not succumb to learned helplessness but take a look at the options that are actually available to us.

Chapter 3 says that the difference between the Non-essentialist and the Essentialist is that the former wrongfully believes that most things are important while the latter realizes that most things are not important.

Chapter 4 gives wise advice to select only the few essential things to focus on to let go the rest to avoid wearing ourselves out.

Part II centers on exploring options before deciding to invest in an essential one. Non-essentialists commits to something that he/she regrets later on while Essentialists take a long time to say "yes" because they only want worthy investments.

Chapter 5 instructs us to create a protected space where we can think about the big picture and make decisions and plans that are aligned with our essential intents.

Chapter 6's tips – journaling, exploring the field personally, considering the unusual, and facing the important questions – allow us to gain a better perspective.

Chapter 7 advises us to include play in our life and work because it improves our mood and makes us more creative.

Chapter 8 teaches us to not neglect sleeping because it restores our abilities and enables us to improve the quality of our work.

Chapter 9 helps make the selection of options easier by prescribing criteria: you must rate it 9-10 out of 10, and it must pass both minimum and maximum standards.

Part III concentrates on eliminating the trivial by clarifying purposes and essential intents, saying "no" to distractions, uncommitting to failing ventures, editing tasks and ideas to make more efficient, and limiting one's activities to avoid scattering efforts.

Chapter 10 says that an essential intent is one that is specific yet inspirational. It doesn't have to be wordy because it's the message that matters and not the style at which it's expressed.

Chapter 11 acknowledges that it's hard to say "no" because we are naturally inclined to please others, so it gives several techniques such as using automatic e-mail responses, asking what to deprioritize, separating the request from the relationship, and more.

Chapter 12 makes uncommiting easier by pointing out strategies such as reflecting whether the investment is still worth it, asking one's self whether one is just regretting having wasted so much effort, among others.

Chapter 13 talks about editing one's life by knowing that subtracting sometimes adds to quality, by sticking to the essence of things and removing the rest, and by editing one's tendency to edit or, in other words, to have restraint when trying to fix something that doesn't need to be altered.

Chapter 14 explains that boundaries help protect our plans and energy, and this is done in advance so that it will become easy to refuse something that trespasses our limits.

Part IV gives several methods to make execution of the ideas previously discussed almost effortless.

Chapter 15 says that buffers can be created by overestimating the time we can finish a task by 50% or more, by preparing for extreme conditions, and by asking ourselves the tough questions and preparing for them.

Chapter 16 imparts the insight that removing obstacles to efficiency involves dealing with the "slowest hiker" – the thing or person that is causing delays and problems.

Chapter 17 helps us attain progress through small wins that are measurable, concrete, and visually portrayed.

Chapter 18 is all about forming good habits by paying attention to triggers that cause bad responses and replacing them with desirable ones and by working on developing one good habit at a time.

Chapter 19 makes us productive by releasing our fears, worries, and preoccupations and instead focusing on what is important right at the moment.

Chapter 20 closes the circle by making us think about what is truly important to us and asking us whether we are ready to embark on the path towards becoming an Essentialist.

FREE BONUSES

P.S. Is it okay if we overdeliver?

Here at Readtrepreneur Publishing, we believe in overdelivering way beyond our reader's expectations. Is it okay if we overdeliver?

Here's the deal, we're going to give you an extremely condensed PDF summary of the book which you've just read and much more…

What's the catch? We need to trust you… You see, we want to overdeliver and in order for us to do that, we've to trust our reader to keep this bonus a secret to themselves? Why? Because we don't want people to be getting our exclusive PDF summaries even without buying our books itself. Unethical, right?

Ok. Are you ready?

Firstly, remember that your book is code: "**READ24**".

Next, visit this link: http://bit.ly/exclusivepdfs

Everything else will be self explanatory after you've visited: http://bit.ly/exclusivepdfs.

We hope you'll enjoy our free bonuses as much as we enjoyed preparing it for you!

Lightning Source UK Ltd.
Milton Keynes UK
UKHW011217160919
349872UK00001B/138/P